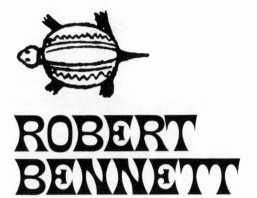

ROBERT BENNETT

By Mary Carroll Nelson

5264

DILLON PRESS, INC.
MINNEAPOLIS, MINNESOTA

Dillon Press, Inc., 500 South Third Street
Minneapolis, Minnesota 55415

Printed in the United States of America

Library of Congress Cataloging in Publication Data

Nelson, Mary Carroll.
  Robert Bennett.

  (The Story of an American Indian)
  SUMMARY: A biography of the Oneida Indian who be-
came head of the Bureau of Indian Affairs.
  1. Bennett, Robert LaFollette, 1912-   —Juvenile literature.
2. Oneida Indians—Juvenile literature.   3. United States.
Bureau of Indian Affairs—Juvenile literature. [1. Bennett,
Robert LaFollette, 1912-   2. Oneida Indians—Biography.
3. Indians of North America—Biography. 4. United States.
Bureau of Indian Affairs]   I. Title.
E99.045N44   970'.004'97 [B] [92]   75-43539
ISBN 0-87518-108-2

ROBERT BENNETT

When Robert LaFollette Bennett, a Wisconsin Oneida,
was appointed commissioner of Indian affairs in 1966,
he became the second Native American ever to hold that
position. Commissioner Bennett's appointment was the
culmination of a career of dedicated service to Native
Americans through his work with the Bureau of Indian
Affairs (BIA) in Utah, Arizona, South Dakota,
Colorado, and Alaska.

While head of the BIA, Robert Bennett worked to open
lines of communication between the various Indian
tribes and the government. In 1969 he retired from
government service and became director of the Indian Law
Center at the University of New Mexico.

Now active as a consultant to both public and private
concerns, and as a member of many boards and
organizations, Robert Bennett has contributed much
to Native Americans and his country throughout his
forty years of public life.

Contents

CHAPTER I

The Oneidas

Long, long ago, the Oneida storytellers say, two brothers built their wigwams in what is now central New York near the place where the Oneida River empties into Oneida Lake. There they raised their families and built a city. In this place, an oblong, rounded stone appeared that was unlike any other stone in the area—a stone with magical powers—and the Indians used it for their sacrificial altar. They named themselves "The People of the Stone" to honor their altar.

The Oneidas became so numerous that they decided to move to Oneida Creek. The Oneida Stone appeared in their new location. Later still, the Oneidas built a village on a hilltop, and the stone followed once more, placing itself in a butternut grove where it has remained to this day. The Oneidas held their meetings and religious services around the stone.

Many years later, when the Oneidas decided to leave the area, they sold their homeland to the people of Utica, New York. The city agreed to preserve an area around the stone to be used as a burial ground for any Oneida Indian who wished to be buried there. When Oneidas return to New York for meetings with other Indians, they often go to see their ancestral home and the granite boulder for which the tribe is named.

The ancient Oneidas lived deep in the northern forest. The women were farmers and raised corn, tobacco, beans, and pumpkins. They also owned the lodges, which were shared by several families. These were oval-shaped buildings made of bark and supported by a framework of bent saplings. The men were hunters, providing the meat and furs for the people, and they were warriors, protecting the fields and lodges. The villages were surrounded by a log wall for defense. In each village there was one large building known as the Long House, where meetings were held.

The Oneidas were one of the Five Nations of the League of the Iroquois. *Iroquois,* the word the French used to describe the league, means "united people." The Five Nations called themselves the People of the Long House. The league inhabited an area of central New York that was thick with trees, filled with fur-bearing animals, and laced by rivers and streams.

For many years, the Five Nations kept peace in the area through an advanced form of government. Each nation had a certain number of chiefs, called *sachems,* who were chosen by the women of the tribe. When a sachem died, his female relatives chose a new sachem from their family. Both men and women voted and expressed their opinions at the Council Fire, which was a meeting of all the nations in the league. These meetings were held several times a year. The tribe desiring a meeting would send out runners to notify the other tribes of the Council Fire. The runners carried *wampum,* which were belts of woven beads that could be read by the Indians as if they were in writing. The message

Iroquois bark house.

they carried told the time and place of the meeting.

On the appointed date, sachems, warriors, women, and children from all the nations came to the meeting place. Usually, this was in the center of the area, the home of the Onondagas, who were called the Keepers of the Council Brand. They stored the wampum and kept a fire burning as a symbol of the league.

Crime was barely known among the Iroquois Indians. They practiced a generosity to neighbor and stranger that is rarely seen in any people. No matter what time of day or night a person visited an Iroquois home, he or she was received with kindness and offered food and shelter. Strangers were welcome for as long as they cared to stay.

Among the men, a talent for speechmaking was thought to be a great gift, for the Iroquois were fine orators. A skillful orator was more likely to become a chief than a brave warrior was, because the orator was able to sway the opinion of the Council Fire members with his words.

To imagine these people living in the northern forests, think of well-built men and women who wore deerskin clothes and moccasins. The men wore shirts and pants in cold weather and breechcloths in summer. The women wore overdresses, skirts, and leggings. All the deerskin was decorated, if possible, with elaborate beadwork. The men shaved their hair except for a scalplock; this kept them from catching their hair on branches as they roamed through the woods. The women wore their hair in long braids. Because of the many trees in their homeland, wood was the material they used most often for their canoes, cooking tools, home-building materials, and bows.

The Iroquois Indians believed in a creator, the maker of all things. They called the creator the Great Spirit. They believed in life after death and in a happy home beyond the sun. The wicked, they felt, would be punished after death. They would go to a dark place where lived the Evil Spirit who created all monsters, poisonous snakes, and dangerous plants. As a part of their worship service, the people sang and danced. Their religion was formal: each person participating in the ritual knew what to do, when to do it, and what it meant. Religion was an important part of the Iroquois life.

Iroquois domestic scene drawn by
Jesse Cornplanter, a Seneca, in 1905.

*Old sketch of an attack
on a fortified Onondaga village
by whites and Indians.*

The lifestyle of the Indians changed with the coming of the Europeans. The Iroquois began trapping for furs to barter with the French and the Dutch, who were the first white people to settle in their territory. In exchange, they received manufactured goods. Most desirable to the Indians were tools, guns, and ammunition.

Control of the fur trade became increasingly important to the Indians as their need for manufactured goods grew. Iron kettles replaced their wooden pots, and after a time the kettles became a requirement for their way of living. The gun replaced their customary weapons, and warriors could not protect themselves with bows and arrows against enemies well supplied with guns and ammunition. Tribes fought desperately with one another for hunting grounds and the opportunity to trade.

The Iroquois fought chiefly with other groups related to them by race and language. Sometimes, persons of other tribes voluntarily joined the Iroquois because they thought that the league was stronger than their own people. So many captives were taken and absorbed into the Iroquois nations that eventually there were few, if any, pure-blooded Iroquois. Their easy takeover of other people added to their strength. After the mid-sixteenth century, when the Iroquois finally defeated the Hurons, the strongest of their enemies, they became the most powerful group of Indians in the area.

The Iroquois did not trust the French, mainly because the French had supported the enemy Hurons. Nevertheless, the Iroquois wanted to sell their furs to the French as well as to the English, who had taken control of New York away from the Dutch. Consequently, the Oneidas were one of the three Iroquois tribes who signed a declaration of neutrality with both the French and the English in 1688. The Onondaga and Cayuga also signed it, but not the Mohawk and Seneca. This is one of the first times that the Iroquois League did not act as one group. The policy of neutrality lasted for years. Neutrality, plus powerful control over their neighbors, insured the prosperity of the league.

The Oneidas were attracted to the religion of the white people. As early as 1702 there was a mission from the Church of England in an Oneida village. In 1709, four sachems went to England and asked Queen Anne for missionaries and schooling in the Christian faith. She had the prayer book and music of the Church of England translated into the Mohawk language, the most widely spoken of the Iroquois dialects. From that time on, missionaries played an important role in the history of the Oneidas.

An Oneida Chief, Skenandoah, was a convert to Christianity and was a close friend of the missionary Samuel Kirkland. These two men were powerful leaders of the Oneidas at the time the Revolutionary War was starting. At a tribal meeting held to discuss the war, Skenandoah stood beside the Oneida Stone on the hilltop and addressed his people. Skenandoah was known as the "white man's friend," because he had saved the lives of many English people when he warned them of attacks by the French and their Indian allies. He could not understand the revolution, and he said that it was like brother fighting brother. Samuel Kirkland also spoke to the Oneidas. Kirkland pleaded with the sachems to take a neutral stand in the war—that is, not to side with either the English or the colonists. Both speakers were convincing. The Oneidas and the Tuscaroras, who had joined the league in 1710, decided to stay neutral. Only later in the war, when their former allies in the league, who had sided with the English, began attacking them, did the two tribes actively side with the colonists. This division of loyalty split the League of the Iroquois, and it never regained its former strength.

By the Treaty of Fort Stanwix in 1784, the new American government gave the Oneida tribe one thousand dollars. The tribe was also granted a small area of land to keep for their own in central New York where the town of Oneida is now. Since they no longer had the whole forest for their own to roam in freely, the Oneidas became farmers, but land buyers wanted to buy even the farmland from them.

During this time, an Episcopal missionary, who was not yet a priest, came to the Oneidas. His name was Eleazar Williams. He found the people divided into two groups: the First Christian Party were those who had been baptized and still believed in the teachings of Samuel Kirkland. The Pagan Party were those who were not baptized and practiced the traditional Iroquois religion. Soon, Eleazar Williams became a strong influence on the Oneidas. He converted the Pagan Party, and on January 25, 1817, they declared before the Governor of New York that they were to be known as the Second Christian Party of the Oneida Indians.

The life of Eleazar Williams is a tale within a tale. Although what follows is partly factual and partly unproved, it is thought to be a true account of this mysterious person whose life was closely tied to that of the Oneidas.

Eleazar Williams had been raised in Saint Regis, New York, as the son of Thomas Williams, an Indian. Thomas's mother was a white woman who married a Mohawk warrior after she had been captured by the tribe. Eleazar did not look like his eleven brothers and sisters. They all had the appearance of an Indian, but he had fair skin, light hair, and hazel eyes.

When Eleazar was a young boy, he suffered from mental confusion that made him unaware of his surroundings. After he struck his head in a fall, his mind cleared, and he became aware of what was happening to him, but he could still not remember his early years. Who he was and where he came from was a mystery to him. The mystery was deepened by terrible scars on his legs, bad dreams, and strange memories. Sometimes he dreamed of a wicked face that he feared but did not recognize, and at times he seemed to remember seeing richly dressed people in a beautiful building.

Eleazar thought of Thomas Williams as his father, but various events made him doubt it. Once he was visited by two Frenchmen who seemed to recognize him and wept when they saw the scars on his legs. At another time he heard his parents talking about sending him and his brother away to be educated. Someone was providing the money to pay for it. He heard his mother say that she would not mind if "the strange boy" was sent away, but she did not want to send her son John. These things troubled Eleazar, and he wrote of them in his journal.

There were also two trunks in the possession of the Williams family. They were filled with medals, clothing, and mementos belonging to people of wealth, and they seemed to have come from France.

During his boyhood, it was arranged for Eleazar to receive an education. He went to live with a minister's family and took quickly to study and to the social graces. He remained a student for many years, and it was his great hope to become an Episcopal minister.

After he grew up, Eleazar's knowledge of Indian languages and his educated manner made him valuable to the United States government. During the War of 1812 he was asked to be the leader of a group of spies, who could freely go in and out of the enemy territory in Canada and gather information on what moves the British forces were going to make. Eleazar proved to be a brilliant leader. He convinced his Indian friends not to make war against the United States. Before the war was over, he was seriously wounded and was nursed back to health by Thomas Williams.

When he finally regained his strength, Eleazar once again returned to his work in the Episcopal church and was sent to the Oneidas as a teaching missionary. He believed that the Oneidas should move away from their New York home

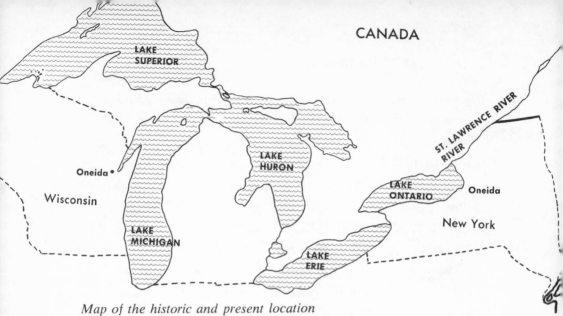

Map of the historic and present location of the Oneida Indian tribe.

and establish a new home in the west, where he hoped that the League of the Iroquois could be restored. Therefore, he persuaded the leaders of the tribe to sell their land and buy new land from tribes in the west. With a group of Oneida chiefs, he set out by canoe in 1821 to the land of the Menominee and Winnebago on the far side of Lake Michigan. The Oneidas made an agreement to buy a strip of land near Lake Michigan that was eight miles wide and twelve miles long from the two tribes. They returned to New York and told the tribe of their plan. There was some opposition, but eventually the people agreed. Eleazar went to Washington to talk to James Monroe, the president of the United States. President Monroe arranged the sale of the New York property and the purchase of the Wisconsin property near the area of Green Bay. In 1823, the first group of Oneidas moved. By 1825, Eleazar had constructed a small log church in the new town of Oneida, Wisconsin. In 1826, he became a minister at last.

Much as Eleazar had hoped for a new League of the

Iroquois, his wishes were not to be fulfilled. Gradually, though, most of the Oneida tribe moved to the new home. Those who did not choose to move there went to Canada. By 1831, Eleazar's influence on the Oneidas was waning. He retired from his mission and went to live at Fox River in the farmhouse of his wife's people, but he still wanted to serve as a minister. He began traveling back and forth to the New York area where he had grown up, trying to establish schools and churches for the Indians there.

While he was on one of these trips, he met someone who told him that the French Prince de Joinville was in the United States and was on his way to Wisconsin to see him. Eleazar hurried to take a boat back across the Great Lakes to his home and found to his surprise that the prince was aboard the same boat. The prince seemed startled when he met the minister and studied his every action and facial expression. When the boat landed at Green Bay, Wisconsin, the prince made arrangements to spend some time with Eleazar in a hotel.

After they were alone, the Prince de Joinville explained that Eleazar Williams was actually the Lost Dauphin, or crown prince, of France. He was the son of King Louis XVI and Marie Antoinette, who were both killed during the French Revolution. He told Eleazar that the dauphin had been imprisoned with his parents and was harshly treated by a guard named Simon. Only through the kindness of a later guard was he smuggled away from the tower where he was held. The child had been so abused that his mind was disturbed, and he appeared to be crazy. A royalist agent had brought him to the United States and placed him with the Williams family in their remote Indian village to keep him safe. Now the new king of France, Louis XVIII, who was Eleazar's uncle, wanted to be sure that Eleazar would never come to claim his throne, so he sent his son, the Prince de Joinville, to meet with him.

The news of his royal birth was a terrible shock to the good minister. The Prince de Joinville put a parchment document on a table for him to read and sign and left him alone to regain control of himself. Then Eleazar read the parchment, written in both French and English. It spoke of him as King Louis XVII and stated that he renounced all claim to his throne and titles in France. Eleazar pondered long and hard on the affair. He finally decided not to sign the paper because if he did, it would mean giving up his birthright. The prince left again for France. It is believed that Eleazar at first intended to go to France and claim what was his, but later changed his mind.

Eleazar Williams continued to live as a poor minister. When he died in 1858, he was buried in the small church in Oneida, Wisconsin. Eleazar never regained complete memory of his life, but once in his later years he was startled by a picture. He said that it was the face of his nightmares. He had recognized Simon, the cruel jailer who had scarred him for life in the tower. Those who knew Eleazar could see his family resemblance to the royal family of France, and they had no doubt that he truly was the lost dauphin. There is a town named Lost Dauphin, Wisconsin, near the Oneida reservation. For the Oneidas, Eleazar Williams was a cherished leader, who had safely brought them to their new home and their religion.

Through the years, the United States government has treated the Oneida tribe both fairly and unfairly. Although never abused as some other tribes were, the Oneidas were deprived of some of their western land. In 1831, the government of the United States took title of tribal land for the Oneidas "in trust" and gave them a section of land that was smaller than the land the Oneidas had originally bought from the Menominees and Winnebagos. Thus, the Oneidas were really cheated by the government, and it was not until years later that they were given money to make up for their loss.

From 1822 until 1880, the Oneidas lived much as they had in their old New York home. They retained their language, customs, and organizations. They continued to farm, hunt, and fish, but they no longer lived in their wood and bark houses; instead, they adopted the housing of the white people. They did not make their clothes from deerskin, but wore white people's clothes. The Oneidas joined the two churches in the community, the Methodist and the Episcopal. They were adaptable people, who got along well with their European immigrant neighbors. They did not have a reservation style of life; it was more like a small town.

In 1887, the General Allotment Act was passed, by which the government divided up Indian lands. Each tribal member over eighteen years of age received a small portion of land. The policy of the government at the time was to send young Indians to boarding schools at some distance from their homes. The goal of this policy was for the Indians to absorb the white people's culture and forget their own.

In 1918, the government began taxing owners of the small land parcels. Before that decision, Indians did not pay taxes on their reservation land. When the new tax regulation was put into effect, the government made up a list of Indians who did not know English. Anyone on the list was excused from paying taxes because the government had the idea that an Indian who could not speak English could not earn enough money to pay taxes on his or her property.

But what of the Indians who could speak English? They were the ones who had gone away to government or missionary boarding schools and had learned the ways of the white people. The government now expected these Indians to be self-supporting, but the Indians were unable to support themselves. It was not enough for them to learn to speak English. They needed jobs and good salaries. Nearly half of the tax-paying Oneidas lost their land because they did not have money to pay the tax.

Our story begins a few years before the tax regulation was put into effect. It concerns one family in the small group of Oneidas who lived in their Wisconsin village in the early years of the twentieth century.

CHAPTER II

An Oneida
Boyhood

Fred and Lydia Bennett, Robert Bennett's parents, met at the Whittenberg School, a boarding school for Indians. Lydia was working for the school as a seamstress at the time. She had attended the school and had finished the ninth grade—a rarity for an Indian girl in those days. Fred, a young man from Pennsylvania, taught agriculture and ran the farm that fed the children. Fred and Lydia were married at Whittenberg in January 1912. Shortly afterwards, Lydia brought her new husband to her home in Oneida, Wisconsin. She owned a portion of the land that had been divided up among the Oneidas by the government. Since she had been to school, she was one of those who would be expected to pay property taxes when the new law came into effect.

The land was too swampy to farm, so Fred went to work for neighbors in the Norwegian Settlement, so-called because the people there had originally come from Norway. After a time, he got a job in Spooner, Wisconsin, at the Agricultural Experiment Station. Fred was not happy with the job because he had to stay in Spooner during the week and return home only for weekends. When the chance arose, Fred became the rural mail carrier in Oneida. He no longer had to live away from home, but he drove thirty-two miles a day by horse and buggy. It took between eight and sixteen hours a day to deliver the mail, depending on the weather. In winter, the roads were so bad that he would arrive home nearly frozen.

The Bennetts' first child was born on November 16, 1912. They named him Robert LaFollette Bennett after a famous senator from Wisconsin. Their daughter, Prudence, was born on October 15, 1913.

Lydia Bennett had a close friend whose baby, a little girl named Helen House, was born about the same time as Robert. Her friend died after the baby was born. The Bennetts raised Helen almost like a twin to their son.

Robert Bennett had light-colored hair, but his skin was dark. Living in Oneida at the time was a black man named Billy whose hair was white. Relatives began calling the Bennett boy Billy, too. Some people, who have known him since childhood, still call him Billy.

Reaching out towards others was a way of life for the Bennett family. In the mailboxes along his route, Fred Bennett would sometimes find a page torn from a mail order catalog with some pictures marked and some money with it. After he returned to the village post office at night, it might take him two hours to make out orders for those on his route who could not read and write. He would fill out the money orders, get them in the mail, and then prepare the change to leave in the boxes the next day.

Lydia often made soup and had Billy take it to families in which someone needed care. She also acted as an interpreter for the neighborhood. Most Oneidas did not speak English. She went with her Oneida friends and relatives to court, to the doctor, or anywhere they needed her. It was not the custom for them to pay her, but when they butchered meat, they would send some to the Bennetts. If they baked bread, they would send up a loaf. Meantime, the Bennetts served their neighbors in many ways.

Soon after their marriage, Lydia had sold her land, and the family had moved into the village. Fred and a few friends formed the Oneida Telephone Company and installed a few telephones; one of the first was in the Bennetts' house. From then on, any person who had an emergency used the Bennetts' telephone to call for help. Lydia usually did the calling for them. After Fred bought a car, he often used it to take people to the hospital.

The Bennett home was a center of social activity. Fred, Lydia, and their friends loved to dance. When they went to the dances, all the babies would be brought to the Bennett house, where Billy and Helen took care of them. There was not a lot of money, but the family was at least as prosperous as their neighbors or more so. The Bennetts knew everyone in the little town.

At home, the Bennetts spoke English. Fred Bennett and the children could understand Oneida, but they could not

Bob and his sister Prudence, and their mother, Lydia Bennett.

speak it. They were used to speaking English, although their Oneida relatives all spoke Oneida to them. In remembering his childhood, Bob Bennett says, "As small children, we could make our wishes known to our uncles and grandparents by one means or another, and we enjoyed visiting with each other."

Fred Bennett took an active part in the town's life. He was the umpire for home games of the Oneida Indian baseball team, and Billy was batboy and mascot. Father and son were close. Young Billy helped out with the work, and he was always ready to rub down and feed the horses when his father came back from his route. Sometimes, when his father was cold and weary, Billy and his mother would have to help him out of the buggy. By the age of twelve, Billy would drive occasionally for his father.

Lydia Bennett believed firmly in the value of a good education. She often said, "You're going to have to get along in this world understanding English." Her attitude was different in every way from that of her mother, Mary.

Mary Doxtator had been brought before a judge because she had refused to send her children to school. Mary and the judge had a long conversation with the help of an interpreter. She told him that Indians needed to know how to get along with one another in the woods and on their own farms—they did not need to speak English or to go to school. Like a true Iroquois, Mary understood that a good way to keep the peace was by discussing all sides of a problem thoroughly. Finally, she proposed her bargain. She would send her four youngest children to the white people's school but keep her four older sons at home. At last, realizing that he was not going to change the mind of this determined woman, the judge agreed. Lydia had been one of the children who had been sent away to school.

Unlike her mother, Lydia realized that her children were already in the world of white people, not in a world exclusively Indian. She looked into the schools of the area. There were three choices. The children could go to the Indian school, the public school, or to the Catholic school, Saint Joseph's. Although the Bennetts were not Catholic, she decided to send her children to the Catholic school. Billy went there for six years and had completed the eighth grade by the time he was twelve.

There was no local high school, so the boy rode seven miles each way on the train each day to attend the ninth grade in Seymour, Wisconsin. For the next year and a half, he went to Saint Norbert's Catholic Boarding School in De Pere, Wisconsin. It is easy to see that the Bennetts valued education for their children.

When he was living at home, Billy was able to take piano lessons with his mother's help. Samuel Bell was the only person working at the government agency office in Oneida, and Lydia did the laundry for the Bell family. Each day Bell came to the village from Green Bay by train and rode

Bob with his classmates at Saint Norbert's School.
Inset, *Bob was known as "speedy" Bennett*
on the basketball team.

back again each night. Billy would pick up the family laundry at Bell's office and take it home. His mother would wash and iron it, and Billy would take it back to Bell. In exchange, Bell gave lessons in classical piano to young Billy, thus inspiring a lifelong fondness for music in the boy.

Lydia and the children had other jobs as well. They joined other Oneidas in the summer in Door County, where they picked cherries. Dormitory housing was available for the pickers. Lydia became a supervisor in this summer work. When Helen reached school age, she was enrolled in a government boarding school at Tomah, Wisconsin. Each summer she came to live with the Bennetts.

The children in the area started working early. By the time they were nine years old, they were thinning and weeding beets. They put in a ten-hour day and earned only sixteen cents an hour. This may sound sad to those who cannot remember the Great Depression. Actually, such low wages were not unusual during that time, and the people were happy to be able to earn any money.

Lydia also worked for a big packing house in Green Bay. The Johannes Brothers Packing Company paid the family for a kind of work that had an enjoyable side to it. In the evenings, the company would drop off sacks of freshly picked beans. Family and neighbors sat talking together while they snipped off the ends of the beans. Then they packed them back into the sacks that would be picked up again in the morning.

There was a pickle factory in Oneida, and the local people picked cucumbers for it. Each fall the youngsters were let out of school for a two-week "potato vacation" to dig potatoes. They also dug beets and cut the tops off them. Strawberries were another crop that needed picking in that area, and the pickers got a part of what they picked to take home.

Whites and Indians alike worked at these jobs, and there were no racial tensions or discrimination. Even in the Depression, many Oneidas had good jobs. They were expert woodsmen, and some men worked up in the wooded northern areas for the lumber mills. The Indians in local schools numbered only 1 percent of the population, but they fit in with everyone else and were not especially conscious of being different.

Billy's father died in 1927 when the boy was in his junior year in high school. No longer Billy, the towhead, he was now young Bob Bennett. For two months, the fifteen-year-old stayed home, helping his mother, but then she wanted him to go on with his education and arranged for him to go to Haskell Institute, a free, government-run boarding school in Lawrence, Kansas.

Haskell Institute was very different from the rural world of Oneida, Wisconsin. Here, the students were all Indians, and they came from every section of the United States. Many of them had been at Haskell for years already and knew the way to get along. Bob Bennett quickly caught on and made friends. It was at Haskell that his consciousness of what it means to be an American Indian developed.

CHAPTER III

Leaving Home

The student body at the Haskell Institute was as large as the total Indian and non-Indian population of Bob's hometown. The eleven hundred students were grouped according to age, and the school was operated along rigid military lines. Rules were strict, and punishment was harsh. This was an entirely different way of life for Bob. At home, he was used to the informal style of family living, and the small number of Indians in the town lived alongside their neighbors.

The school started with the first grade and continued two years beyond high school as a junior college. Though Bob arrived in his third year in high school, he met boys and girls there who had begun in the first grade.

Try to imagine yourself, if you can, leaving home at the age of seven to attend a strict boarding school with a short annual vacation. You were not allowed to speak your native language or to practice your native religion. You would find it hard to hold on to your family ways and tribal traditions.

Bob's strong attachment to his family and hometown, however, combined with the fact that he entered the school at age fifteen, made his position at Haskell different from that of many of his fellow students. He did not feel so cut off from his roots as they did, and he was ahead of students of his age in school. Bob was a well-built, sturdy boy, who was used to hard work. He was friendly and eager to learn about the school. Luckily, he met some Menominees and Oneidas he had known in Wisconsin. Their familiar faces made the school seem less strange.

First, Bob learned to march. The school was organized by squads, platoons, and companies. Girls as well as boys marched from one place to another in lines at Haskell. There were separate dormitories for girls and boys. Students who broke the rules, including those about language and religion, were put in the disciplinary barracks, a kind of jail. On Saturdays, boys in the disciplinary barracks had to work in the stone quarry.

The students who had been at the institute since their early years formed a strong pressure group—that is, they knew the rules well and wanted everyone to follow the rules so that there would not be any trouble. In this way, the students forced conformity, and there was not much rebellion.

The highest ranking student position was that of colonel, and any student achieving this rank was much admired by the others. While Bob was not at Haskell long enough to be promoted to colonel, he did win the respect and friendship of his fellow students, many of whom have continued to be lifelong friends.

Bob remembers the school well, especially the food. During the Depression, Haskell was allowed only twenty-six cents per day to provide a student with meals. Gravy was served three times each day to make the meal more filling.

The students did not go hungry, but there was little variety to their diet.

Every fall, the boys went rabbit hunting to provide a meal for the school. Armed with sticks, four or five hundred of them walked down to the Wakarusa River. They made a huge circle in the fields and began closing in the circle. Using this ancient Indian technique, the boys caught enough rabbits to feed eleven hundred people a Sunday feast!

No use was made of all the rabbit skins in spite of the traditional Indian skill with furs. Indian arts and crafts were not taught at Haskell Institute or at any other government boarding schools in those years. It was the policy of the government to encourage the young Indian to forget his or her own culture. Bob Bennett, as the second generation in his family to attend government boarding schools, was far removed from his Oneida ancestors. Bob was learning new ways for a new world. In his future, there would be little need for ancient skills. Since his childhood was like that of small town non-Indian boys, Bob first experienced the government's policy towards Indians at Haskell Institute. Although he wanted an education, he doubted the wisdom of the policies in force at the institute and wondered how he and his fellow Indians should react to them.

The teachers at Haskell expected their students to be silent. Although they preferred class participation, they knew that Indians do not like to be singled out. An American Indian is not competitive in the way that other Americans are. When public school teachers ask a question, usually several eager hands will go up—the students want to answer. Bob liked to speak up and was accustomed to it.

At Haskell, he began by raising his hand to answer questions, but he soon stopped because he noticed that other students were not putting themselves forward. After a week, he behaved as the other students did.

The government paid the student's way home only every four years or upon graduation. Since Bob did not have the money to go home, he spent his summers at Haskell working on farms nearby. One summer, while he was away working, the boys' dormitory was remodeled. When he returned to school in the fall, all of his clothes were lost except the ones he was wearing. Fortunately, he had his summer wages, so he bought new clothes.

Music continued to be an important part of Bob's life. He and a group of friends went to see the superintendent of Haskell to request permission for school dances. Bob played piano in the school concert orchestra that performed for the first dances. Later, two dance bands were formed, and Bob played in them. The leader of one dance band was Carroll Martell, a Chippewa Indian, who became an architectural engineer in later years. Carroll's sister, Lucille, also went to Haskell. Bob began to see Lucille when he could get some free time.

A year and a half after Bob entered Haskell, he finished high school, but he did not leave the institute. He remained

Bob (third from left) with friends at Haskell Institute, and his high school graduation picture.

another two years for training in the business department. Bob was graduated from the junior college in 1931.

During his last years at Haskell, the military system ended, and Bob saw the beginnings of student government. Each floor of the dormitory was called a lodge, and the students were allowed to give their lodges Indian names. Members of the lodge elected their own officers. The government's change of policy was, in part, the work of John Collier, who tried to reform the Indian Field Service in the Bureau of Indian Affairs. John Collier was a non-Indian who was commissioner of Indian affairs from 1933 to 1945. His philosophy emphasized self-determination for Indians. The changes John Collier brought about were to influence Bob Bennett's policies when he worked for the Bureau of Indian Affairs.

There was much on Bob's mind in those early days of the thirties. The country was deep in the Great Depression, and jobs were hard to find. Luckily, there was a need for a clerk right at Haskell Institute. George Shawnee, who had been in the first class to graduate from Haskell Institute, was the chief clerk there, helping to manage the office. He hired Bob Bennett for one dollar a day. Bennett stayed on as a clerk in the office. He continued to play in the orchestra and the dance bands, and he saw Lucille when he could.

The next summer, the Indian sanatorium in Kayenta, Arizona, sent a request to the school for a summer replacement clerk to help out while the regular clerk took a needed vacation. Bob was chosen to go.

The sanatorium was an isolated hospital. It cared for people who were suffering from tuberculosis, a highly contagious disease. In those days, sulfa drugs had not yet been developed, and providing bed rest and good food was all that could be done to help patients with tuberculosis. It was a very serious illness. The sanatorium also cared for people with birth defects and other health problems so severe that they could not take care of themselves. Just as Haskell Institute had been a shock to the small town boy, so the sanatorium deeply affected the healthy young man, who had had little contact with seriously ill people before.

Bob worked as a clerk in the dispensary, the department which made up and gave out medicines. Sometimes, people at the sanatorium died of tuberculosis. When a patient was near death, the doctors had the patient moved to a room in the dispensary just behind the door in Bob Bennett's office. He often heard the death sounds of patients so close to him. There was a reason for this strange system. Many tuberculosis patients were Navajo Indians. At the time, the Navajos believed that death brought evil spirits. If a patient died in a regular hospital room, Navajos would never enter the room again because they felt that the place where a person died was inhabited by ghosts, and they were afraid to stay in such a place. If no relatives came to claim the body, the dead person was buried in the cemetery of the sanatorium, and Bob helped with these burials.

In addition to his clerical duties, Bob Bennett had other jobs at Kayenta. Navajos who could not read asked him to help them with their orders from the trading post. He walked to the post, which was about a mile away from the sanatorium, about three times each week to turn in the orders. In a way, he was doing what his father had done for the Oneidas years before as a rural mailman.

Every night, silent cowboy films were shown to the patients. Andy Devine, an old-time western star, helped arrange for the movies to be shown. Andy was one of the many actors who spent time on the nearby Weatherall Ranch. The ranch was often used as a set for western films. Since there was little in the area other than the sanatorium, the actors became acquainted with the patients and the staff. Impressed by the needs of the Indians, the actors supplied movies to the sanatorium to entertain the patients.

Bob went over to the Weatherall Ranch in his free time and talked with the men who worked there. Once, when Andy Devine was vacationing at his home in Flagstaff, Arizona, his studio asked him to drive up to the ranch and check it out as the site for the movie, *Laughing Boy*. Bob met Andy during that visit. Andy wanted him to have a part in the movie, but the film had to be postponed for a year because of lack of money. Bob was unable to stay in Arizona long enough to be in the movie, so Bob Preston, who later became a prominent Navajo leader, was cast as the hero's friend—the part Bob was to have taken. *Laughing Boy* won a Pulitzer prize for its author.

At the time of taking the summer job at the sanatorium, Bob Bennett was undecided about what he wanted to do with his life. Just nineteen years old, he learned a great deal during this time with the Navajos. He felt compassion for the people he met and for the patients he helped. His experiences had a deep emotional impact on him and helped him to decide what his life work was to be. By the time he returned to Haskell in the fall, Bob was sure that he wanted to enter a life of service to his people, not just the Oneidas, but all the Indian people.

CHAPTER IV

An Officer of
the Ute Tribe

A few months after Bob returned to Haskell Institute, he was offered a job as junior clerk on the Ute reservation at Fort Duchesne, Utah. Bob moved to Utah in March 1933. He was twenty years old, and his career in the Bureau of Indian Affairs had begun. The BIA is the federal agency that administers government programs having to do with Indians. It provides several different kinds of services such as education, housing, employment assistance, and land management. It is directed by the commissioner of Indian affairs.

Since he was a bachelor, Bob was assigned living quarters in a building that had been used to house unmarried army officers. He soon made himself at home in the community. He joined the Ute basketball team and became its manager. The team played local games and in state tournaments. He formed his own dance band, and they went to nearby towns to play. Although the trumpet and sax players could play well, they did not know how to read sheet music. Bob bought sheet music and patiently played it for the rest of the band until they had learned the music by ear.

Bob was not a bachelor for long after he moved to Utah. Later that year, he made a brief trip back to Lawrence,

Kansas, where he married Lucille Martell, the girl he had met at Haskell. The wedding was celebrated in Saint Joseph's Church with a flock of Martell relatives present. Not having time for a honeymoon, the young newlyweds went immediately to Fort Duchesne. They moved into an eight-room frame house, formerly officers' quarters. The large, drafty house was hard to heat. The furnace gobbled up a thousand pounds of soft coal every five days. Bob had to carry all the coal in, and all the ashes out.

At first the couple found the old house too big, but soon they began to have visits from Lydia Bennett, Bob's mother, and Lucille's relatives, too. The first of the Bennett children to be born was a boy, who died after only a few hours— an event that was especially sad for young Lucille. The family grew, however. John was born in 1935; William arrived in 1936; and Leo, in 1938. These early years of the Bennett marriage were happy ones.

There was a camp for the Civilian Conservation Corps on the Ute reservation. CCC camps provided a way for the government to employ people during the Great Depression. The workers did jobs in the forests in many parts of the country. Since there was a need for more people at the camp in Utah, Bob sent for two of Lucille's brothers and some of his Haskell friends. A few of them remained with the Indian service throughout their careers. They married Ute women and eventually returned to the reservation when they retired.

Bob spent these years learning as much as he could about the tribal government and the problems of the Utes. One person who helped Bob gain knowledge and experience was the superintendent of the reservation, Lewis W. Page.

Page was unusually advanced for his time in the methods he used to carry out government policies. Instead of issuing orders and demanding that they be obeyed, he explained government policies in leisurely meetings with tribal leaders. He listened to the Indians' opinions and answered their questions carefully. As a clerk, one of Bob's duties was to go to the meetings with Page and take notes. Page's manner of dealing with tribal affairs impressed Bob and influenced his own style of administration in later years.

The Utes began to trust Bob Bennett—so much so that they asked him to go along with them on their hunting and fishing trips. Bob listened to their stories while sitting by their campfires at night. His relationship with the Utes deepened as he came to understand them.

He still remembers well a story told by an old Ute chief, Sapanies Cuch. At a meeting with the White River band, the discussion concerned putting out poison to get rid of the prairie dogs. The chief spoke against it:

> Years ago there was very tall grass on the prairie. The government let white men run sheep on it. Then, a few years later, all the grass was eaten away. The government blames the prairie dogs. But, the same spirit put us here who put the prairie dog here. I would no more poison the little prairie dogs than poison you or me.

The story illustrates the Utes' belief that all of nature is related and that the earth is their mother. Bob interpreted this story in the light of Ute traditions. The Utes are linked together by a common language, but they have always lived in separate bands. There are six bands in all. At one time,

Ute bands roved over an area that stretched from Salt Lake City to Denver. Before the white people's interference, it was their custom to travel widely, hunting and gathering what they needed for food, clothing, and shelter. They have never been farmers.

Through the General Allotment Act of 1887, the government required that the agricultural land on Indian reservations be divided among tribal members so that Indians would farm their own land. Although the policy was meant to make them financially independent, it went against the Utes' traditions and angered them. They did not believe that anyone could divide up or own pieces of Mother Earth.

The White River band in Colorado was more angry than the others. The government agent, a man named Meeker, was supposed to enforce the government policy on the band's territory. He tried, without success, to make them farm. When he dug up their racetrack in order to divide it into farms, members of the White River band killed Meeker and captured his wife and daughter. Tim Johnson, the leader of the kidnappers, was just a boy then. The government caught the men responsible for the crime. Mrs. Meeker and her child were rescued and given a lifetime pension. There was a trial, and the men were made to return to the reservation. The entire band, in fact, was forced to move to Uintah Basin on the Utah reservation, far away from their former home. Later, they ran away to live with the Oglala Sioux in South Dakota, but they were back in Utah when Bob Bennett lived in Fort Duchesne.

Bob met Tim Johnson, who was an old man at the time, and they became friends. At Haskell, Bob had been a classmate of Tim Johnson's son.

*Bob with Jim Thorpe, one of the greatest athletes of all time,
who also attended Haskell Institute.*

Even in Utah, the White River band did not take to farming. At first they just rented their farms to settlers and collected a fee each year. Later they took up cattle raising. This business was less confining than farming, and all the Utes preferred it. They took over their farms again only to raise hay for their stock to eat. Each of the Ute families had some cattle, but in their meetings with the government agents and with each other, they realized it was impractical to run their cattle separately. Each of the three bands on the Utah reservation formed its own live-stock association and ran all the cattle together. When Bob Bennett was serving in Utah, the three bands chose him to be the secretary-treasurer of their livestock associations and their annual United Bison Industrial Convention. He took notes at their meetings, kept track of how many cattle each person owned, and saw to it that each received the correct amount of money after the cattle were sold.

A major change in government policy that deeply affected all Indian tribes occurred in 1934—the Wheeler-Howard Act. It provided for each tribe to set up its own government and constitution if it so desired. To explain this act to the Utes, Lewis Page made many trips to meetings with tribal leaders of the three bands. Bob went too.

Although Bob was not a Ute and despite the fact that he was a BIA officer, the Utes wanted him to serve as the secretary-treasurer of the tribe. Bob signed their constitution as a tribal-elected official. The three bands on the Utah reservation formed one constitution and set up a tribal government in which each band would have two representatives. This representative system by bands continues today on the Ute reservation.

Thirty years after Bob helped the Utes form their government, the tribe built a motel and had a big celebration
for its formal opening. Many leaders of the state and federal
governments who were friends of the Utes were invited to
sit on the stage for the ceremony and to introduce themselves to the audience. One by one, the guests gave their
important titles and their names. Finally, Bob Bennett stood
up. He had acquired many titles that he could have used,
but all he said was his name and "I was tribal clerk." The
Utes gave him the biggest hand. He was not only a servant
of the government, he was also their friend. This is what
he always remembered, and it is what the Utes remember
about him still.

CHAPTER V

The Ladder
of Experience

In 1938, Bob Bennett was transferred to Washington, D.C. During his five and a half years of service
on the Ute reservation, Bob had carried out governmental
policies. Now he was given an opportunity to work in the
main office of the Bureau of Indian Affairs where those
policies were made. This change in jobs was an upward
step for Bob.

The Washington office dealt with matters involving Indian lands anywhere in the United States and Alaska. Any
tribal problem that concerned land—sales, leases, or the
uses of land or water—was solved in that huge office. Working there gave Bob a larger view of Indian affairs.

The director of the office was James M. Stewart. Stewart encouraged Indians to work up to higher-ranking jobs
within the Bureau of Indian Affairs, but to qualify for promotions, they had to go to law school. Bob was already
working on semilegal matters because almost all tribal land
problems were covered by a regulation or a law. To solve
the problems, he was required to know these regulations.
Though he had had only two years of college, he also had
over seven years of experience on the job. At that time
it was possible to enter law school without graduating from

college. Bob began attending law school at Southeastern University. Law school is difficult, and to succeed at it, a person must concentrate on study. Bob, however, could not devote his entire life to school. He had to work a full day at the office. For two years he went to school two hours each morning before work and studied at night. After he graduated in 1941, he was qualified for further promotions.

James Stewart had become director of the agency on the Navajo reservation at St. Johns, Arizona. He asked for Bob Bennett as his administrative assistant. The family moved west again. In those days BIA employees and their families lived in government housing on the reservation. The Bennetts' three boys went to a reservation grade school. One of Bob's first actions at St. Johns was to sign up for the draft since World War II had begun.

Stewart took Bob with him to many meetings with the famous Navajo leader, Chee Dodge. Dodge was the first modern leader of the Navajos, and he was an elderly man when Bob knew him. He had once been an interpreter for the army and was able to understand governmental methods. He liked and respected many white people and had quickly learned efficient ways of doing things from studying those with whom he worked. Dodge used advanced methods of breeding livestock on his own land and had developed the finest herds on the Navajo reservation. He readily shared his knowledge with other Navajos. Dodge was respected as a business manager by both the whites and the Navajos. He served as the first elected tribal president and was re-elected until his death.

Chee Dodge believed strongly that Indians had to accept

Chee Dodge (at the microphone)
at a Navajo meeting.

the education offered to them by the whites. He repeated
this idea in many speeches before his people. Education,
he felt, offered the only way for Indians to progress. Bob
Bennett was impressed by Dodge's views. They reminded
him of his mother, Lydia, who had worked so hard, years
before, to keep her children in school. The era of his grandmother was over—it was no longer justified to scorn the
white people's school.

At the meetings Bob attended, both Chee Dodge and
James Stewart were always careful to explain their thoughts
and the government's policies to the Indians. It is the Navajo
way to act only if there is unanimous consent. Chee Dodge
patiently explained, listened, and talked with his fellow Navajos until understanding was reached. Stewart worked
closely with Dodge and the Navajo people. Stewart and
Dodge were models of the kind of official Bennett admired
—men who believed the role of an official was not to gov-
ern, but to lead.

Chee Dodge liked Bob and often asked him to drive

when there were district meetings to attend. On the twenty-five-thousand-square-mile Navajo reservation, these meetings were held in widely separated districts. (Unlike the Utes, who are organized into bands, the Navajo people are organized into geographical districts.) During the long drives Bob became a close friend of this fine man.

Bob also got to know other Navajo leaders. At the tribal meetings he took the minutes and, once again, served as secretary-treasurer. He helped write up resolutions for the tribal council to discuss. Working with Dodge, he introduced the idea of a fixed agenda for meetings. Dodge liked to put the least controversial issues on the agenda first to get them out of the way early so that there would be plenty of time to discuss troublesome subjects that might require many hours of talk in order to reach a unanimous decision.

Bob also met the younger Navajos. Once more he joined a dance band and a basketball team. With these two groups he was able to meet many young Navajos socially. In the three years Bob served as Stewart's assistant, he became a familiar, trusted friend to many of the Navajo people.

World War II was at its height in November 1944 when the Marine Corps issued a call for two hundred Navajo men from Arizona. The marines wanted Navajos to work in their secret code section. By speaking in their native language, the Navajos could keep secrets from the Japanese and pass along necessary information that no one else could understand. Bob could not speak Navajo, but since he was an Indian registered for the draft in Arizona, he was called up. In a sense, his being drafted was a mistake, but he had to go anyway.

Bob moved his family to town. While he was away in

the service, his family was no longer eligible for government housing on the reservation. The children changed schools again. Bob left for duty in San Diego.

In his training platoon Bob served with Navajo men. One member of his platoon was Peter MacDonald, who later became the Navajo tribal president. They were friends in the service and have remained so. At the end of the training period, Bob was awarded a certificate as the most outstanding recruit in the platoon. He had become an expert rifle marksman. When the other men went off to serve in the code section, Bob became the clerk of the court for General Courts Martial. Although he was only a private, Bob was given this job because he was a law school graduate. He had men working for him who were of higher rank.

When Bob was released from active duty in 1945, he went back to work with the BIA and was the district supervisor stationed in Fort Defiance, Arizona. He resumed his friendship with Chee Dodge and visited him in his home in Crystal, Arizona. He helped Dodge with tribal affairs,

Bob (far left) with other Indian servicemen as charter officers of the American Legion Post on the Navajo reservation.

and when Dodge grew tired during tribal council meetings, he sometimes went to Bob's office to rest.

Bob organized and was commander of the American Legion Post for the Navajo tribe. Once again, he helped the Navajos make arrangements for their dead. As commander of the legion post, he requested permission from the Navajo Tribal Council for a cemetery to be reserved for burying Navajo veterans, and he arranged the military funeral services for deceased veterans. In a military funeral, the American flag is used to cover the coffin, and after the service it is presented to the family. Sometimes the relatives refused to take the flag. Understanding their fear of close contact with a dead body, Bob knew that they did not intend any disrespect for the person who had died or for the flag. His own traditions did not prevent his taking part in funerals and he was glad to perform this service for the Navajos in addition to his work at the BIA office.

Bob left the BIA temporarily to work with the Veterans Administration. He helped prepare special programs for Indian veterans so that they could take advantage of their veterans' benefits. The benefits were provided by an act of Congress, called the GI Bill by most peopie. Because of this bill, veterans could go to school. Bob traveled all over the area to find eligible Indian veterans. Then he had to find school programs to match each veteran's needs. If he could not find a school program to benefit the veteran, he would create one by finding the teacher, the building, the equipment, and the student. Bob made speeches to any interested groups in Arizona. He told of the needs of the Indians for education, housing, and health care on the reservations.

While serving with the Veterans Administration, Bob and his family lived in a rented house ten miles outside of Phoenix. In Phoenix, Bob joined the National Congress of American Indians. This important group was the first organization founded by Indians that represents all Indians. Bob was the program chairman for their annual convention. He contacted Indian leaders throughout the country to serve as speakers. Each year he traveled to distant meetings at his own expense and managed the conventions. It was this experience that enabled Bob to meet nearly all the national leaders of Indian tribes. His friends in the National Congress of American Indians supported Bob throughout his career. He is still a member of the congress.

In 1947, Chee Dodge died at the age of eighty-six. Bob had visited him in the Ganado Hospital during Dodge's final illness. He went to Fort Defiance for the burial ceremony and was asked to serve as a pallbearer. Bob called on Navajo veterans to act as the other pallbearers. Because of their wartime experience with death, they were not hesitant about participating in the funeral. Dodge was given a military funeral service since he had once served in the army years before as an interpreter. None of the older Navajos would touch the casket, but they felt the loss of Dodge deeply. Dodge had led the way from the old era to the new. For Bob Bennett the death of Chee Dodge meant the loss of a fine friend.

Two years after Chee's death, the Bureau of Indian Affairs asked Bob to return to the service and move to Aberdeen, South Dakota. The BIA was beginning a new program in which Indians on reservations were to be trained for city jobs so that they could learn to adjust to town living while learning a trade. After their schooling was complete, it was hoped that the Indian veterans would find jobs and remain in the city. In this way opportunities would be opened for Indians to enter off-reservation life. The Bennett family had added another person to the family by the time the move to Aberdeen came. Their new baby, Jo Anne, had been born shortly before they left Phoenix.

During the years in Aberdeen the family grew to six children. Dave was born in 1950, and Robert, Jr., in 1951. Soon after the boys were born, Lydia Doxtator Bennett, their plucky grandmother, died. She had been the major influence on Bob Bennett's beliefs, and her passing saddened him.

Since early in their marriage, Lucille Bennett had occasionally been too ill to care for her family properly. As the years passed, these times occurred more frequently. Bob relied on the older children to keep things going. Because they had moved often, they had learned to adjust well to many situations. The older boys could take care of the little children for a few hours when Bob was in town and could get home at night. If Lucille was ill when Bob had to go on trips, he asked her mother or her sister to take care of the family for him, and one or the other stayed with the children and looked after Lucille.

In 1951 Bob was called back to Washington, where he worked to develop tribal programs for the education and employment of Indians. This tour lasted for three years, and then he was ordered to Colorado. Bob was back with the Ute tribe again, this time as superintendent of the Consolidated Ute Agency in Ignacio, Colorado, for two years.

Among the programs Bob started in Ignacio was his plan

*Superintendent Bennett (in corner) with
the business committee of the Southern Ute tribe.*

for awarding money to any Ute family with a practical plan for its use. Almost every family thought of some money-producing way to use the available dollars. People call this sort of program "seed money" because by giving a small amount of money for a good purpose, much can grow from it. Bob was trying to teach the principles of economics to the Utes so they could become financially independent. Bob met with Ute council leaders in both Utah and Colorado to explain the plan. He saw many of his old friends again on these extensive trips.

In Ignacio, as he always had before, Bob made an effort to get to know the people in his new community. He served on the board of directors of the Chamber of Commerce and was charter president of the Lions Club.

In 1956, Bob returned to Aberdeen, South Dakota, for the most responsible position he had yet filled. He was the assistant area director and remained in this assignment for six years. The BIA was new in the town of Aberdeen. Although Bob had served there before, it had not been in the same type of office. He was in charge of setting up a new area office which would supervise the activities of the various BIA agencies in the area. Among Bob's concerns was the social life of his office personnel. Nothing had been organized when he arrived, so he formed the first social club for the staff. The club put on parties and dances, and Bob played the piano at these events. There were both Indians and non-Indians on the staff. Bob served as president of the club and presided at the farewell parties for those who were leaving the office, welcomes for those who arrived, Christmas parties, and so on, all in an effort to keep morale high.

Bob also formed a bowling league and a golf league for BIA people. The golf tournament he founded for BIA groups in the Dakotas and Nebraska is still held each year.

There were two reasons why these social activities were important to the employees. Since the BIA transfers workers every few years, these activities helped newcomers feel at home. They also encouraged cooperation and understanding within the BIA staff so that it was an efficient office. Good executives always try to look after the welfare of their personnel, and Bob excelled in his efforts.

As assistant director, Bob traveled constantly to oversee the large area. One of his biggest tasks was to help organize the Pick-Sloan Flood Control Project. By the terms of this project, the tribes were given money to help with flood control on their lands. Bob met with the tribal leaders as they tried to plan the best use of the money.

One by one during these years John, Bill, and Leo graduated from high school. As his turn came, each boy had a long talk with his father about his future. The three older boys chose to go into military service first and to college later. John joined the navy for a four-year tour of duty and then he attended Arizona State University at Tempe, Arizona. Bill went into the navy, too, and then to the University of Arizona at Tucson. Leo went in the marines and then to the University of South Dakota. The boys have all become successful businessmen.

Bob's greatest wish for his children was that they would grow up strong and independent, and he has been rewarded by having that wish fulfilled. Because of his wife's illness, Bob often had to act as the children's only parent. His way of being a father was similar to his way of being a BIA official. He respected his children, and because he took time to explain his rules to them, they always knew what he expected. He listened to their opinions and talked with them. The sharing and communication they had within the family kept their morale high even though they had to move around often and be self-reliant.

CHAPTER VI

Alaska

Bob's career in the BIA continued upward, and he was honored for his work by those he served. In 1962, the Indian Council Fire awarded him the Indian Achievement Award, a distinguished honor.

The year 1962 was a saddening and yet exciting year for Bob. He and Lucille were divorced during this time, and Bob was given custody of the three children still living at home. Shortly afterwards, he was asked to go to Alaska as the area director for the Alaska region. Bob and the children moved to Juneau.

As always, Bob took an active interest in his new community and joined the Juneau Rotary Club. While he was directing a variety show for the organization, he met Cleota Minor Brayboy, who was also directing a theatrical production. Cleota was a social worker specializing in child welfare. She was working for the BIA in the high school of Mount Edgecombe, a boarding school with 650 students in Juneau. She also worked with the Tlingit Indian families in the area. Bob and Cleota were married in December 1963.

This marriage added a wealth of happiness to his life and to the lives of his children. Cleota was trained in relating to the social and emotional needs of young people.

The three younger Bennett children welcomed the friendship and understanding she offered, and she became a major
influence on their development. Jo Anne and Cleota became
especially close. Bob had gained a helpmate in the raising
of his family. The high position he filled in the BIA had
social obligations, and Bob could now entertain more and
more of the visiting government officials and native people
in his home.

Bob was now responsible for a huge area, and in Alaska
he dealt with several distinctive groups of native people.

The Eskimos live mostly on the northern coast and tundra, an area that sweeps from the Aleutian islands off southwestern Alaska across Canada to Greenland. The tundra
is a vast plain where the climate is so harsh that trees
cannot grow. Under a thin layer of top soil that thaws
in the summer, the ground is always frozen.

Arriving on the North American continent later than
the ancestors of the American Indians, the Eskimos resem-
ble the people of northern Asia with their brown skin, wide
faces, and high cheekbones. The Aleuts are sometimes spoken of as the "cousins" of the Eskimos since they also have
Asian racial characteristics. They live on the Aleutian Islands, the chain of islands that extends into the Pacific, and
on the southern coast of the Alaskan peninsula.

Indians live in the pine forests south of the tundra. The
Tlingit and Haida Indians live in the southeastern panhan-
dle area. They belong to the northwest coastal tribes that
inhabit Canada and the lower United States. In the interior,
Athabascan Indians, with a simple culture, continue to hunt
and fish.

In order to meet the native peoples of Alaska, Bob had

*Bob with a group of Eskimo students
leaving Mount Edgecombe School in Sitka, Alaska,
for summer vacation.*

to travel over an area almost one-fifth as large as the rest of the United States. From east to west, Alaska is 2,300 miles, and from north to south it is 1,400 miles. Because there are few roads and no passenger trains, almost every Alaskan town has an airfield. Bob visited outlying settlements in a small airplane, big enough only for the bush pilot and one passenger. As Bob traveled around Alaska, he visited some Eskimos who still made their home in igloos, which were round houses made of iceblocks. He stopped by the shacks that are found in all the little fishing towns and old buildings whose architecture still reflected a Russian design.

Alaska used to be known as Russian America. It was owned by the Russians until 1867, when the United States bought it for $7.5 million in gold. For years, Alaska was a territory, at first governed by military officers and later by a governor appointed by the president. The territory had a legislature of its own, but its decisions had to be approved by Congress. When Alaska became a state in 1958, William A. Egan was elected governor by the people of the new state and remained in office for seven years.

The BIA was responsible for the native population, but the relationship between the government agency and the groups in Alaska developed differently from that with Indian tribes in the rest of the country. The government of the United States had defeated most American Indian tribes and then had made treaties with them individually, in which certain Indian rights and guarantees were outlined. These treaties have often been broken, but at least they acknowledge the sovereignty (nationhood) of the Indians. Treaties gave Indians a position in some ways close to that of a foreign country. The government had agreed that each tribe had its own leaders who could make demands on the government for their people. When Alaska was bought from Russia, the United States government made no agreements with the native people living on the purchased land.

So long as the land was part of the territory of Alaska, it was protected, more or less like a huge park, although there were local governments as well as private ownership of land in the territory. The federal government was involved in Alaskan affairs through fifty-two agencies. Facilities such as highways, schools, hospitals, and transportation were paid for by the federal government, not by local taxes. Immediately after statehood was won by the people of Alaska, the federal government gave the new Alaskan government the right to choose 103 million acres to keep as state-owned land. Some of the lands chosen by the new government were those traditionally occupied by the native peoples. They were badly frightened. How would they live if they had to move? If they could stay, how would they pay taxes? They had little money, and with statehood came the need for taxes. The population of Alaska is so small that each citizen would have to pay steep taxes to support the state. It was a serious problem for everyone, but more so for the natives.

During his first few years in Alaska, Bob became aware of the fears of the native peoples. He knew the feelings they had about their land, and these people were his responsibility. He followed his custom of talking things over with them. This is why he traveled so much. Remembering the ways of men he admired, such as Page, Stewart, and Dodge, Bob listened more than he spoke. Then he explained what was happening under the new government.

After he had studied the problems of land ownership, Bob recommended to his bureau that all transfers of land to the State of Alaska involving traditional settlements of native peoples be frozen. No more land could be chosen by the state under such a freeze order. His recommendation went to Washington to the secretary of the interior, Stewart Udall. Udall issued the freeze order. The Eskimos, Aleuts, and Indians were pleased by the order because their homes were no longer threatened.

Others in Alaska were not happy with the freeze. One of those who was less than happy was Walter J. Hickel. Hickel was a self-made millionaire, a legendary figure in Alaska. He had arrived as a penniless youth in 1940. Within ten years he owned the Hickel Construction Company of Anchorage. His company owned housing developments, apartments, hotels, and shopping centers. He began the company by building a house himself and selling it at a profit and then doing it again and again. Hickel was interested in land. He wanted the population of Alaska to increase and to have more industry move to Alaska so that there would be more jobs. Hickel had strong views about the development of Alaska's oil resources, which were known to be under the North Slope, the traditional home of many Eskimos. It is understandable that Hickel would take a different position on the freeze order than Bob did.

Like Bob, Hickel was destined to rise in government, and the controversy that began in Alaska would later reappear when the two men occupied positions of authority in the nation's capital. Already politically ambitious, Walter Hickel began his race for the governorship of Alaska. The conflict between BIA policy and the platform of Hickel's supporters grew wider. Hickel became Governor of Alaska on December 5, 1966.

Bob's tour of duty in Alaska had ended a year earlier. During this troubled time he had developed a new style of administration in Alaska, based on personal contact and as much conversation as needed to insure understanding.

Most Americans are in a hurry. Business conferences begin abruptly, last as little time as possible, and end quickly. Most Indians do not consider this polite. A visit with an Indian begins with quiet conversation on many subjects so that both people feel relaxed. Only after these courteous exchanges have gone on would it be polite to bring up the reason for the visit. The need for following this form had impressed itself on Bob, especially in his contact with the Navajo tribe. An instinct for these small, but important matters made it possible for him to develop friendship and trust between himself as an officer in the BIA and the people he was to aid. Bob's concern for native peoples, his courtesy, and his understanding of their etiquette were well-known to both the native population and the BIA.

Bob often dropped in by bush plane to visit many out-lying places where there was only a one-room school with a lonely teacher. These teachers were hired by the BIA in the lower United States. Their fare to Alaska was paid for them. If they stayed two years, they also got free trans-portation home. Those who signed up for another two years were given a free trip home and back to their school. The lonely life caused many to drop out before their time was up. Bob tried to show his concern for the teachers by keep-ing in touch with them in person. His hope was to improve their morale by listening to their problems and trying to solve them. There were more than a hundred schools in Alaska run by the BIA at one time or another. Bob suc-ceeded in his effort to make the teacher's life a better one. Fewer teachers quit early during his service than before.

He had a firm policy that he has never changed. No matter how often he traveled, he always cleared up all out-standing business on his desk before he left. "I always leave my desk clean," he says. He read, answered, dictated, and signed all mail. He made the decisions he was authorized to make and saw the people he needed to see. In short, Bob did all the work that only he could do, and yet he still visited more settlements than any area director had before him.

It is easy to see why this man was selected by the sec-retary of the interior, Stewart Udall, to come to Washington, D.C., to be deputy to the commissioner of Indian affairs. Udall was in the Cabinet of President Lyndon B. Johnson. It was Udall's clear intention that Bob Bennett would suc-ceed Dr. Philleo Nash, commissioner since 1961.

CHAPTER VII

Commissioner of Indian Affairs

In January 1966, the Bennetts moved to a home they bought in Bethesda, Maryland. The three younger children were in high school. Cleota became a clinical social worker at the National Institutes of Health. She worked with children who had severe heart ailments and their parents, and she completed a research study on the patient-physician relationship.

Bob reported for work at the BIA. He was immediately aware that his role was a sensitive one. Stewart Udall, secretary of the interior, was critical of the way the BIA had been administered by Commissioner Philleo Nash. He made his views known. Dr. Nash wanted to continue in his job as commissioner. Feelings ran high. All correspondence began to come directly to Bob from Secretary Udall, bypassing Commissioner Nash. Bob always took it in to Dr. Nash to maintain a good working relationship with the man who was over him. As public criticism against Nash grew, Bob's position became more difficult. This situation lasted until Dr. Nash resigned from his job on March 19, 1966.

Three days later, President Lyndon B. Johnson, on the advice of Stewart Udall, appointed Robert L. Bennett to the post of commissioner of Indian affairs. Appointees to such top positions must be approved by the Senate. The committee, headed by Henry M. Jackson, the senator from Washington, held a hearing in April 1966. The committee wanted to know about Bob's views on important issues and government policies.

Bob was asked how he felt about the BIA policy on termination. Termination means the ending of government protection of a tribe. After termination, the tribe is completely self-governing, the way a town is, and must pay for its own facilities. There are tribes who have asked for termination and then have found it hard to survive without the financial support and other commitments of the federal government. Bob answered the question this way:

> When and if any tribe has progressed to the point where it is comparable to the surrounding area, economically, socially, and politically, I will report that fact to the Congress. Then the issue of termination would be a matter for Congress and the tribe to settle.

This was a good answer to a tricky but valid question. Bob and the committee members knew that many years would have to pass before an Indian tribe would be in the same economic condition as its neighborhood. Although Indians were progressing fast, the rest of society also was progressing, and so the gap continued.

The senators discussed the large amount of money, $1.5 billion, that had been appropriated during the six years of the previous commissioner's time in office. They were disturbed that the Indians were still at the bottom of the educational and economic ladder. Bob promised that within three months he would give them a written report, telling them about the ways in which he planned to reduce the "red tape" in Indian affairs so that it would be easier for Indians to be heard and express their views. He said, "I will do my best to eliminate the destructive effects of paternalism." Bob was speaking of the manner in which the BIA had been treating Indians—as a parent treats young children, rather than treating them like responsible adults.

Rules and procedures that hindered the bureau's work had built up over many years. The BIA had been formed on June 30, 1834, to take care of all relations with Indians. At first, it was under the War Department, but on March 3, 1849, it became a civilian bureau under the Department of the Interior. In the treaties between the government and the Indians, the Indians gave up their land, and the government agreed to provide them with services. These services grew more and more expensive as the Indian population increased and its poverty worsened. As the BIA policies changed, more regulations were added to those already in effect. It was Bob Bennett's hope to simplify the rules and give more responsibility to the Indians.

Indian leaders around the country began contacting the Senate committee and asking that Robert Bennett's appointment be confirmed. The Senate confirmed his appointment unanimously on April 13, 1966. On April 27, 1966, he was sworn in at a ceremony at the White House with Cleota and the children watching proudly. President Johnson promised to support Bob in his efforts to advance the Indians' progress. In the speech he gave at the ceremony, President Johnson said, "Bob Bennett is going to be one of the greatest Indian Commissioners that the United States. . . has ever known."

Bob's sons Bobby and David, his daughter Jo Anne,
Secretary of the Interior Stewart Udall, Bob and Cleota Bennett,
and President and Mrs. Johnson, at Commissioner Bennett's
swearing-in ceremony.

Only one other person of Indian blood had ever held the job of commissioner before Bob. He was Eli Samuel Parker, a Seneca Indian, who was commissioner from 1869 to 1871. During the Civil War, Parker was an aide to General Ulysses S. Grant, and he himself rose to the rank of general. General Parker played an important part in writing the surrender terms that ended the war. When Grant was elected president in 1865, he appointed Parker to the post of commissioner of Indian affairs. Parker had ideas that were too advanced for the politicians of those days, and he stayed in office only two years. While Bob was commissioner, he paid a visit to Eli Parker's home in Tonawanda, New York, out of respect for his predecessor.

When Commissioner Bennett called his staff together, he told them his plans and desires. It was obvious from his remarks that he wanted to do away with the bureau's paternalistic treatment of Indians. This is a summary of the points he made.

1. He would not question the staff members' ability to do their job because he already knew they were qualified.

2. The Indian leaders were to be partners in decision-making and in carrying out decisions affecting them.

3. He had complete confidence in the Indians' ability to be partners with the BIA.

4. He wanted two-way communication between the Indians and the government. He was going to act not only as a supporter of government programs for Indians, but also as a representative of Indians within the government. Formerly, the commissioners promoted BIA programs down through their staff and out to the tribes. Bob wanted to consult with Indians and tell others in government what they had told him.

5. He wanted the BIA staff to have a pro-Indian attitude.

These ideas from Bob's speech to the staff were printed in a letter and sent out to all the field offices of the bureau.

Bob began the "partner policy" right away by having joint meetings with the BIA staff and Indian leaders. During these meetings he gave instructions to his staff so that the Indian leaders heard him and knew what the commissioner expected from his own workers.

Remembering that time, Bob says, "When I first took over, my Indian friends cooled off, waiting to see if I remained true to my convictions or would be a tool of the administration. The first stance I took was when I appeared before the Navajo Tribal Council and said I would resign if asked to go against my convictions."

After the 5½-hour hearing given by the council, Annie Wauneka, a well-known Navajo leader, came up to him and said, "Bob, you'll do because—after all, we raised you." As the daughter of Chee Dodge, Annie Wauneka had known Bob since his young days on the Navajo reservation. The Navajo tribe is the largest in our country. Its endorsement was a great help to Bob in his new job.

Other people besides Indians were concerned that Bob would be a "yes-man" to those in high positions. Shortly after he began his job at the bureau, a free-lance reporter told Bob, "You only got this job because you're an Indian." Six months later, she came back and apologized. "You're going to be your own man," she said.

In the first few months of his term, Bob traveled constantly to meet with tribal leaders and answer their questions. He asked for and received their views about reorganizing the bureau. Most of all, he wanted to impress the leaders with his intention to make them partners in deciding their own future.

There were times when Bob opposed a policy, but he could not express his opposition because the policy originated higher up in the government than his own office. At such times, he just had to wait and hope that the tribal leaders understood why he did not speak out. What distressed him most was a decision that was legally correct but that was a bad policy because it was against the Indians' best interests. He felt strongly that any government policy that affected the life of the Indian should be presented first to the Indians involved—not issued as an order. He encouraged the Indians themselves to express their feelings about policies with which they disagreed.

The role of commissioner often placed him between the government and the Indians. He did all in his power to keep the lines of communication open so that, by talking over different points of view, both sides would understand each other. Of his job as commissioner, Bob says,

> You must be willing to assume the role of being placed in a difficult position. The hardest person to support in your organization is the one who is right the wrong way. You can always support a man who makes an honest mistake. But a man who takes a supercilious, arrogant attitude might do exactly what the Indians want and still not win their support. Also, the one thing you can't explain is no decision.

There were so many meetings and conferences all day that Bob had to work at home to keep up with it. Every evening he took home two big briefcases and worked from eight to twelve o'clock each night.

Bob visits with two delegates
from an Indian youth organization
in his office in Washington, D.C.

At the same time Bob tried to be a good father during his children's high school years. His position as commissioner required him to entertain important people in government and Indian affairs. Instead of going out all the time, Bob and Cleota entertained at home and included the children so that Bob could spend more time with them. In this way, the young people met high government officials and tribal leaders, as well as foreign dignitaries.

The BIA was a place most foreign visitors wanted to visit on their rounds of Washington. Bob had a chance to meet almost all the visitors from other governments during his time as commissioner. He arranged for them to tour the headquarters. Glass cases of artifacts from tribes all over the country line the halls of the bureau so that it is almost a museum. As a token of their visit, the foreign delegates were given little art objects made by the Indian people.

Among the humanizing changes Bob started was a policy of accepting collect calls from Indians anywhere at any time. Old-timers at the bureau warned him he would be snowed under with such calls, but Bob still told Indian audiences, "I'm never further away than the nearest telephone." There were only three collect calls received during his term. One was from a man who heard him speak and called just to see if he would really answer. Most Indians would rather pay for their own calls if they could, just out of pride, but the word spread that if they wanted to call, Commissioner Bennett would be glad to talk to them.

Indians around the country felt that Bob Bennett's appointment was a victory for their people. Some of the older Indians would shake hands and say, "We have finally won."

An eighty-year-old medicine man and his wife traveled all the way from Montana to conduct a prayer service over Bob right in his office. These personal contacts with the Indian people are cherished memories for Bob.

Other commissioners had conducted meetings with Indian delegations formally. Numerous BIA experts would sit with the commissioner. Secretaries jotted down notes for the records that would be kept. Bob did not work this way. He was alone in his office when he met with Indian groups, and no records were kept. The word spread that Commissioner Bennett's door was open for any Indian who needed to talk to him. Such a personal approach won the confidence of the Indians.

On his travels, Bob had contact with BIA agencies in all areas. Once he was visiting an office when a young Sioux came in to ask for $100. He was a patient in a mental hospital. He was not violent, but he lived permanently at the hospital, for protection. Once a year he went home on vacation to visit his parents. The money, which came from his own property, was managed in trust by the BIA superintedent. Since all the man's needs were taken care of by the hospital, the superintendent did not think that he needed the money. In fact, he thought it would not be a good idea for him to have it, and so he turned down the request. When Bob talked with the man, he found that the Indian wanted to give the money to his parents. It was the custom to give a party for returning relatives, but his parents had no money. Bob persuaded the superintendent to change his mind, and the young man got his $100.

Sometimes, Bob feels, government agents find it easier

Bob Bennett in his office with representatives
of the National Congress of American Indians,
Secretary Udall, Vice-president Humphrey, and
Sarah Jackson, Miss Indian America.

to be technical about rules so that they will not become involved with the Indians in a personal way. By being strict about paperwork and regulations, bureaucrats keep a distance between themselves and the people they are to serve. When this happens, he or she has no understanding of the real problem. The agent is acting more like a stern father than an understanding helper. This again is paternalism.

Bob tells a story to demonstrate the difference between the paternalistic method and the partnership method in running the BIA. There was an orphaned Indian girl who came to the agency and asked for money for food and clothes. Since the girl went to a boarding school, Bob knew that she did not need money for food. Bob had a talk with her, and she admitted that she had given a false reason for wanting money because she was afraid that she would not get it if she told the truth. She really wanted a Pendleton wool shawl—an expensive, but desirable item for an Indian girl—and she wanted to entertain her friends. Bob asked her to put down her real reason on the request and to ask the clerk to show her own financial records to her. As an orphan, the girl received monthly Social Security payments from the government. Bob wanted her to know all about her own money so that she could make up her own mind about how much she could afford. After that, she came in and asked for what she wanted. She told the truth and made her own decisions. She did not have to wait and see if the BIA would decide things the way she wanted. In this way, one girl learned how to handle money, a skill she would not have learned by listening to a government agent telling her she should be more responsible.

Bob spent his years as commissioner building a relationship of trust between his office and the tribes. He also tried to build trust between his office and Congress. He always kept senators and representatives informed of any Indian business occurring in their districts as soon as it happened, so that they heard about Indian affairs first from him. On the basis of this trust, Bob could go to Congress with a request for funds or legislation he needed for the bureau and be assured of a friendly reception.

During Bob's time in office, all the preliminary legal work was done to insure that the Taos Indians of northern

New Mexico would get their Blue Lake back. This beautiful lake has religious meaning for the Indians. They had been trying to regain possession of it for years. It was finally turned over after Bob left office.

While Bob was commissioner of Indian affairs, legislation was pushed through Congress that gave the Five Civilized Tribes of eastern Oklahoma the right to elect their own officials. Previously, the leaders had been appointed by the BIA. Bob talked the appointed leaders into supporting the new rules. Some of them were then elected by their people to fill the new offices.

Bob wanted women to have more important roles in the BIA. Indian women carry on the culture of the tribe, and they are the ones who decide if a child will go to school. They are the ones who retain the old arts and crafts and pass them on. Partly as a result of Bob's encouragement, more Indian women are going into public service.

Improving the American Indian's financial condition was Bob's most powerful commitment. He favored tribes going into business on their own reservations. To do this, he encouraged the tribes to rent their land to private industry. Once the plants were built, there would be more jobs for the Indians. Fairchild Camera and Instrument Company operates an electronic plant built by the Navajo tribe on the Navajo reservation. The BVD Company built a garment factory on the Hopi Reservation. In Madera, California, the Philco-Ford Corporation began a training center to help teach job skills to Indians. Government programs in education, too, are now widely distributed on reservations; Head Start, the Youth Corps, and the Job Corps have had a deep impact on Indian young people.

Bob's strong feelings about the importance of education also had its impact on the BIA. He created a new job at the bureau, called assistant commissioner for education. He appointed Dr. Carl Marburger to fill it. Under Dr. Marburger, the scholarships that allowed Indians to attend college or vocational schools were increased. Whenever Indian children could attend nearby public schools rather than all-Indian schools some distance from their home, they were encouraged to do so. By 1967, Bob could announce that two-thirds of all Indian children were in public schools in their own communities. It is hoped that this program will eventually do away with the need for very young Indian children to attend boarding schools.

Keeping the Indian culture alive was one of the goals Bob had. Indians really want to preserve their own culture. If young parents find jobs off the reservation, they will leave their children with the grandparents. In that way the children will grow up Indian. More children are living with someone other than their parents among Indian people than in any other part of our society.

In order to encourage Indians to keep their tribal culture, the government has provided community buildings on res-

Commissioner Bennett on a visit to a boarding school in Concho, Oklahoma.

ervations to serve as centers of local education and as places where Indian arts and crafts could be taught. Highway building, too, has been emphasized as a way to increase the sales of Indian arts and crafts.

The building of new roads on reservations has helped Indians in several ways. Transportation on reservations has always been difficult. It was one of the main reasons why boarding schools were necessary. Bad roads prevented children from going to school by bus and living at home. Bad roads also contributed to the high rate of unemployment among Indians. They could not get to their jobs easily, and raw materials could not be brought in for Indians to use in manufacturing.

Bob's impact on the BIA was felt in his own office as well as on the reservations. He ruled that the auditorium in the BIA headquarters building was to be open for meetings, including those held by Indian groups who were critical of the BIA. He even authorized publishing the criticisms of these groups and having them distributed. He believed that he was commissioner of all Indians, not just those who supported him. Young Indians today are impatient with rules and with the slow progress of their people. They are calling for immediate changes. They do not support the conservative, step-by-step changes that Bob feels are more practical.

When the Poor People's Campaign marched on Washington in 1966, many Indians joined the protesters. Bob did not want a fight to start that involved any of his race. He developed two ways to avoid a confrontation between the Indians and the government.

1. He did not deal with opposition leaders face-to-face

but used a go-between. In this way, each side could change its position without losing any pride in front of the other. Also, there was no clash between the two sides.

2. He let the Indians carry out their intentions to march and meet. He even let them meet in the BIA auditorium. As long as they did not act in an unreasonable manner, the Indians would be supported. If anyone should get hurt or be sick, the BIA would take care of him or her.

These two policies helped to keep tempers cool. They were based on understanding and friendship even in the face of opposition. The idea behind them was that not everyone has to think alike, and that people should be able to discuss their differences.

Sometimes at a meeting in the BIA auditorium, a critic would come up to Bob as he sat in the audience and shake his hand before going up to the stage and making a very critical speech. As the speaker left the stage, he went up to Bob and shook hands again. The critic was showing Bob that his criticism was not personal. It is important in a meeting with Indians not to show anger or personal feelings. Bob is good at this. He never embarrassed an Indian critic by answering charges or attacking him or her in public. Instead, he just listened. By "keeping his cool," as people say, Bob gave both sides of an argument a fair hearing. As a result of his self-control, he created a new spirit of openness between the Indians and the government.

CHAPTER VIII

Indian
Statesman

Bob Bennett filled the highest job in the BIA for three years. In 1968, a new president, Richard M. Nixon, took office. It is the custom for incoming presidents of a different political party to replace all appointed officials with ones of their own choosing. Resolutions from Indian tribal leaders poured in, asking Nixon to keep Bob Bennett. Nixon did not ask for his resignation.

An old difference of opinion, however, dating back to Alaska days, created an impossible situation for Bob. President Nixon nominated Walter Hickel to be secretary of the interior. The Senate hearing on Hickel's appointment was a long and bitter one. A growing tide of feeling was rising in the country against pollution. Environmentalists were calling for safeguarding our land. Just as he was about to be questioned on his viewpoint, Hickel made a remark that he was against "conservation for conservation's sake." He felt that saving land, just to save it, was against progress. There was an immediate outcry of criticism against him. The senators questioned him hard and finally made him promise that he would uphold the former secretary's freeze order against assigning any more of Alaska's lands to state ownership for the next two years. Hickel had to agree to this order even though he was very much against it. At last, his nomination was confirmed, although not unanimously.

Hickel took office. Under him was Robert L. Bennett, the man who had recommended the freeze order in the first place. Hickel did not speak with Bennett at all. All communication between the two men was indirect. The situation was like the one with which Bob had coped when he was deputy commissioner except that now he was the person being bypassed. Bob wanted to finish the programs that he had started in the BIA. He knew that the Indian tribes felt at ease with him and wanted him to continue as commissioner. He also knew that he could not fulfill his office without the cooperation of the secretary. On May 31, 1969, Bob resigned and retired from government service after thirty-eight years of duty.

Bob began to get job offers from private industry and accepted a temporary post as a consultant to a foundation specializing in training programs. A short time later, he accepted an appointment as director of the Indian Law Center of the University of New Mexico Law School.

The Bennetts bought a lovely home in Albuquerque near the Manzano Mountains at the eastern edge of the city.

Bob began his new job on February 1, 1970. He worked hard at developing the staff and program for the law center. The center seeks Indian students who are interested in becoming lawyers, and it is overwhelmed by applications. Bob's plan was to turn over the director's job to a younger person. In the spring of 1973, such an individual was chosen —Philip (Sam) Deloria of the Standing Rock Sioux Tribe and a graduate of the Yale University Law School.

*Robert Bennett and a descendant of Chief Joseph
at a ceremony marking the issue
of the Chief Joseph stamp.*

*Commissioner Bennett in his office
in Washington, D.C.*

Bob at the piano, with jazz trombonist
Russell Moore, a Pima Indian, playing together
at an Indian Fair.

Despite his long service, Bob has not been able to retire and relax. Several times a month, he drives or flies somewhere to consult with someone or to give a lecture. He maintains an office at the university and still has an active role as a consultant to the Indian Law Center.

Still concerned with education, Bob is advisor-consultant to the School Board of the Southwestern Indian Polytechnic Institute of Albuquerque. He is also on the board of Arrow, Inc., the National Advisory Council on Indian Youth. He is an advisor-consultant to the all-Indian Board of Regents of Haskell Indian Junior College. He enjoys the activities of Haskell's alumni club in Albuquerque, and he keeps up with his old friends as well as the younger graduates. He was selected as an outstanding graduate and presented with a lifetime membership in the Haskell Alumni Association. In addition to these activities, he is consultant to the William H. Donner Foundation, Inc., of New York. He is still a member of the American Legion and the National Congress of American Indians, and he also maintains his membership in several professional organizations.

Bob does not feel that older leaders should continue to dominate Indian life, and he says that it is time for the younger ones to lead. He does not intrude in an Indian meeting unless he is asked to attend or to be on the program. His position is like that of an elder statesman. Many young leaders come to visit him at his home to ask his opinion privately on a variety of issues.

In his own family, Bob has children with two different lifestyles. His older sons are all successful businessmen in the world at large. The younger three grew up in the socially conscious era of the sixties. Like others in their age group, they hope to find their own identity and use their talents for personal enrichment rather than strive only for financial success. Jo Anne, for example, is a fine dancer, swimmer, and skater.

Having a big family with different interests gives Bob an understanding of a new, young group of Indians and non-Indians. He feels a vital concern for the country now that many social institutions are being questioned and, in

Bob and Cleota Bennett at home in Albuquerque, New Mexico.

some cases, undergoing changes. The Bennett family is still close. They keep in touch by frequent visits and correspondence. Bob feels that he must not interfere with the lives of his children, but he wants them to feel welcome in his home and to come to him if they need anything.

Throughout his forty years of public life, Bob has contributed much to the development of Indian people. His service to them has been varied, and his experience wide. With his knowledge of the way our economy works, Bob sees the steps Indians must take to find their way into an independent economic future. He believes that education and a satisfying job are the answers to an Indian's hopes for a better life. With the wisdom of a seasoned statesman, he realizes that today's Indian youths no longer want to take part in the mainstream of America. They want to share in America as Indians, maintaining their own identity. Bob has dedicated himself to paving the way for those who will follow.

Robert LaFollette Bennett can look back and be pleased with the service he has given and continues to give to his race. By his own efforts, he climbed the ladder of government as far as it would take him. For Bob, serving others with understanding was his goal. In spite of all his success, his goal has not changed. He continues to serve.

THE AUTHOR

Mary Carroll Nelson has a bachelor's degree in fine arts from Barnard College and a master's degree in art education from the University of New Mexico. She is an elementary school teacher and a professional artist, as well as a writer.

Ms. Nelson is a member of the National League of Pen Women in Albuquerque, and she has written articles for periodicals such as the *New Mexico Magazine, American Artist, Artists of the Rockies, Today's Art,* and *Lady's Circle.* She is the author of *Pablita Velarde, Maria Martinez, Annie Wauneka,* and *Michael Naranjo,* other titles in *The Story of an American Indian* series.

The photographs are reproduced through the courtesy of Robert Bennett, the Green Bay Press-Gazette, *Minneapolis Public Library, Smithsonian Institution, and U.S. Department of the Interior.*